Letters to

My Brother In Law

Letters to
My Brother In Law

Bill Leitzy

To order additional copies of this book, contact:
Xlibris Corporation
1-888-795-4274
www.Xlibris.com
Orders@Xlibris.com
104297

Dear Brother-in-law,

I have been meaning to write you for quite some time; however we have been very busy since moving to town this spring. Your sister had been after me to plant a blue spruce tree in the back yard, so as a surprise I ordered one from the nursery here in town. It cost me a hundred dollars plus the planting but she was very pleased so what the heck. After it was planted I watered it faithfully but it soon started to turn brown and the needles started falling off from the lower branches. I complained to the man I purchased it from at the nursery and he came out to check it. He said I think you have a tom cat in the neighborhood using this tree, I can tell by the way it looks. What you need is a larger tree with branches at least three feet above the ground; I have a beautiful Japanese maple I can let you have for about one hundred and fifty dollars more money, however it will be next week sometime before I can bring it out.

So while waiting for the new tree I decided to get even with that cat. I baited a mouse trap with a sardine and placed it near the spruce tree, the trap was gone the next morning. Later in the day I was talking to the neighbor who was working in his yard and he proceeded to tell me how his pet cat came home to be let in the house and it had a mouse trap caught in his whiskers. He said his cat must have gotten into it down by the river because he really smelled fishy.

When the new tree arrived it really pleased your sister, but several days later she informed me there were scratches on the trunk of the tree. That evening I sat in the patio watching the back yard when the neighbor's yellow tom cat went directly to our new Japanese maple and started sharpening its claws on the trunk. I was extremely upset to say the least, so the next morning I got a five gallon bucket and dug a hole in the yard directly under the new tree and buried the bucket to ground level. I then filled the bucket about three fourths full with water and added some Easter egg coloring that was left over from last year. I also dumped about a half gallon of turpentine in the bucket and stirred it up and covered the top with some old window screen and sprinkled some grass over the screen. We had just caught a mouse in the garage that morning in a trap, so I fastened toothpicks on his legs with scotch tape to make him stand up. But his head still hung down because of a broken neck and I again fixed that with a toothpick by sticking it down his throat. I had some trouble doing that with only two hands since your sister refused to hold his mouth open for me. Then I stood him up on top of the grass covered screen over the bucket. He looked darn good considering what that mouse had been through, his eyes bulged out a little more than normal is about all.

That evening I watched from the patio and finally here came the cat heading straight for my tree. He stopped and hunched down when he saw the mouse and started to thrash his tail several times before diving on the mouse. He disappeared from sight for a moment then he came up out of the bucket like he was shot out of a cannon, it was a sight to behold. It looked like a rainbow with four legs and a tail shooting out of the ground.

Several weeks later while talking with my neighbor, he told me that his pet cat had disappeared but another cat that was a female kept trying to get in his house all the time. I asked him how he knew the cat was a female, and he said it was a three colored cat and they are always females. Several days later he told me his pet cat returned the morning after a bad thunderstorm went through the previous night, wasn't that a big coincidence?

I went to the nursery I bought the tree from and told the man about how my tree got damaged. He told me I should get some "pine tar" or black roof patching to coat the trunk of the tree to help it heal. I covered the whole trunk form the ground up to about twenty inches high, thinking bad thoughts about cats all the time I was doing it. Then just last week I saw a furniture truck delivering some new furniture over at the neighbor's house. Several days before that I saw them getting new carpet. Thinking they must have hit the lottery or something I went over to admire the new furniture.

The neighbor proceeded to tell me he had let his cat in the house the other night before he discovered the cat had black tar all over his feet. Before he could catch the cat he had climbed on the couch and three chairs, not to mention walking all over the carpet in two rooms. Well I could see he was not in the mood to be asked what he did with the cat; however I have not seen the cat for several weeks now.

Well I guess it is time to close for now, sometime I must tell you about my other neighbor that has a barking dog that does not know when to shut up.

Your sister says to tell you hello and to come over sometime to see her new tree. We are getting adjusted to living in town and getting to know our neighbor's fairly well.

Sincerely,

You're Sisters Husband

Dear Brother-in-law,

I think that I mentioned in my last letter about one of my neighbor's here in town having a dog that barks constantly. Maybe I should clarify that a little because it really is not a bark like a normal dog, I would classify it more as a yip. Now I normally like dogs and I have had many over the years and was quite attached to several of them. But this dog I am starting to hate with a passion, as he never stops yipping when he is tied outside, and that is much of the day. He just looks at the house and apparently wants back in and he keeps it up until he does get back in the house.

I got to thinking if there was a way to get that dog to yip inside the house like he does outside, they just might get rid of him. At night I see him quite often looking outside through the window. I got to thinking about a small flashing light that operates from a battery that I had picked up at a flea market last year. I think it was made for a bicycle, anyway I fastened the light to a long cord about seventy five feet long and tied a rock to the other end. I waited until it got dark and threw the rock as high as I could over a limb of our Sycamore tree in our back yard. I then tied another cord to the light before hoisting it high in the air. I then brought the line I had just fastened to the light through the open patio window and sat down to wait until the neighbors went to bed. About ten thirty the lights went out; however there was a night light on in the room with the window that the dog usually looked out of.

About eleven thirty I saw the dog jump up with his paws on the window sill and look out, I immediately started to swing the light back and forth. Eventually it started to swing in a huge circle flashing all the time; I could see the window in front of the dog starting to fog up from his yipping. I was enjoying myself immensely for about twenty minutes, when the back door opened up and my neighbor came out in his pajamas. He was barefoot and had his pipe in his mouth, smoking as usual. He stood watching my swinging light for a few seconds, then started down the hill in his yard faster than I have ever seen him move before, looking up at the flashing light all the time. I never gave a thought of this happening and I was desperately trying to come up with some kind of logical explanation for the light.

I could see him clearly from the street light in the front of the house. Now he has an old garbage can lid in the yard that he uses to put shelled corn in when he feeds his four ducks. He never saw the lid as he had his eyes on my swinging light the whole time, when he accidentally stepped on the lid and it slipped on the wet grass. One foot went with the lid and the other foot went higher than his head as he proceeded to land on his back with a resounding thud. His pipe flew out of his mouth and almost landed in the pond. That incedently was the first time I ever saw him without a pipe in his mouth, and I saw that he just laid flat on the ground not moving or anything.

Now I don't like to brag, but I feel I am pretty good in a crisis situation when the need arises. So I immediately rushed out of the patio and took down the line and retrieved my light and threw it into the patio before he regained consciousness. Then I ran over and checked his pulse and then discovered he was not breathing, quickly I rolled him over on his stomach and applied systematic pressure on his back. There was no way I was going to give him mouth to mouth the way his breath smelled from all his pipe smoking.

He finally groaned and I rolled him over on his back and sat him up, and the very first thing he said was what happened to my pipe. Then the second thing he said was, did you see that U.F.O.? I said no I just came out to get a breath of fresh air and I saw you lying on your back in the grass. I asked him if he thought he was all right and he said he thought so, then he asked me if I would go look for his pipe. I found his pipe over by the pond next to a big duck dropping, not wanting the evening to be a complete waste; I shoved the duck dropping down into his pipe and took it back to him. He stood up and reached into the pocket of his pajamas and retrieved his tobacco and matches and filled his pipe and lit it. He proceeded to take a big drag and exhaled, after which he said to me you know I think it's about time I consider changing my brand of tobacco, as this stuff is starting to taste a little like shit.

I slept like a baby the rest of that night, the next day your sister wanted to know where all that string came from in the patio and I said that I had found it out in the yard; probably a darned squirrel carried it in from some place. Oh yes, I almost forgot to tell you, your sister came in the other day from talking to our pipe smoking neighbor. She thinks he is starting to get a little funny because he was going on about seeing a U. F. O. over our house the other night. She also said he has developed quite a limp and walks kind of hunched over. I said he is probably developing arthritis from walking around at night barefoot in the wet grass.

Till next time;   you're Sister's Husband

Dear Brother-in-law,

Do you remember in my last letter to you I was writing about my neighbor with the barking dog and his ducks. Well last week he had a bit of an accident and he lost his car in a fire. And it took place just a couple of blocks from our house, he was really lucky or maybe I should say he was very fortunate that he was not badly injured.

Maybe I should start back at the beginning and explain how it all happened. We have so many squirrels here in town and I decided to start trapping some and take them out to the farm, and release them. I placed the trap out by the old sycamore tree between the two rubber geese that your sister puts out in the yard ever summer. It was one of those so-called humane or live traps that are legal here in town, I think. Without using any bait I have caught four squirrels so far this summer. Then one day I looked out and saw something white caught inside my trap. Upon further investigation I discovered that it was one of my neighbor's ducks that was caught in my trap. While I was standing there looking at the duck in my trap that was sitting between the two rubber geese your sister had put out, I got a brainstorm. My neighbor wasn't home so I could use the pond in his back yard for my planned idea.

I am sure you have seen the television show "America's Funniest Home Video's" where people send videos in for the chance of winning cash. Well I got a camera as a present last Christmas and decided that this was my golden opportunity to try it out. I proceeded to cut the legs off one of the rubber geese that had its head sticking up like it was looking for something. I shoved the duck inside the rubber goose through a hole that was in the bottom. I left his legs stick out of the bottom and carried the whole thing with me to the house so I could get my camera. That was a mistake because I had to clean up the kitchen floor from the duck, but I needed a kitchen knife so I could cut a small opening in the rubber goose about where the ducks eyes would be so the duck could see where it was going.

I set the rubber goose on the pond and it took off like one of those "wave runners" you see up at Lake Erie. I started the video camera but I had trouble holding it still because I was laughing so hard watching that rubber goose try to catch up with his buddies. The only trouble was his buddies did not know he wasn't a big goose that was chasing them and they were trying to get away from him as fast as they could. They made about two circles on the pond and then lit out across the yard, trying to get away from the goose that was chasing them. I was sure I had a prize winning video in the making when it suddenly dawned on me, how in the heck was I ever going to catch up with those ducks, with my gimpy knees and all. They ran out in the street and then proceeded to go right down the center. The three ducks were going side by side and the big rubber goose bringing up the rear trying to catch up with his buddies. I tried to keep up with them as best as I could, at the same time using my camera taking in all the action.

About a half block past a four-way stop, wouldn't you know they met my neighbor coming home in his car and he was about to have a head-on collision with his own ducks. He was driving fairly slow and when he saw he was about to run over his own ducks he swerved his car instead of braking. His car jumped the curb but fortunately he came to a stop before hitting a house. Unfortunately the reason he came to a stop, was he had hit a tree in the yard.

I noticed he was not hurt, only shook up a little and so during the commotion I was able to catch the duck that was in the rubber goose and pull him out without anyone seeing me. I was able to hide the rubber goose in a mailbox close by on the street corner, and then went back to the accident scene; my neighbor was telling the policeman about how he saw a goose chasing his ducks down the street. When the policeman glanced over toward me I took my forefinger and pointing to my head I made a circular motion. He smiled and nodded his head up and down before writing up a ticket. Then he said I will have to smell your breath for alcohol, and I saw the officer cringe when he did that because my neighbor is a chain pipe smoker. I think I told you before this guy is never without his pipe, but I noticed that he did not have it with him now. I soon found out why, as smoke started to come from his car. The officer then used his radio to call the fire department. I guess when he hit the tree his pipe fell down between the seats and caught one of the seats on fire. He came out of the ordeal quite well because he is now driving a new automobile and smoking a brand new pipe. But do you know what? I was in so much of a hurry when I got my camera to shoot the duck scene; I forgot to load my camera with film.

Several days after this took place your sister wanted to know what happened to one of her rubber geese that was out by the tree. I had forgotten all about the goose I had put in the mailbox, so I went down to the Post Office and asked if they had a package shaped like a goose without a return address on it, sure enough the postman came back with your sister's rubber goose. He told me there was no address or return address on it and besides there were no postage stamps on it that he could find. I told him my wife said something about sending a package to her brother in Florida, and must have forgotten to do that. The postman said their automatic sorting machine must have done a little damage as there is a slit in the neck and the legs seem to be cut off. On the way home I threw the thing in a dumpster that was sitting in the alley and now I know what to get you sister for her birthday that is coming up soon.

Well I had better close for now, besides I see the ducks are in our yard again, and I have to go and chase them out, they are getting to be a big pain in the neck

Till next time;   you're Sister's Husband

Dear Brother-in-law,

Remember in my last letter I told you about my neighbor that has four ducks that are always over in our yard. Well your niece was home for the weekend and she has a friend that had good results keeping ducks confined by stretching a string about eight inches high around the area she wanted to keep her ducks in. The next day your sister and I put string up between our yard and our neighbor's yard eight inches high just like we were told. But the ducks apparently did not know they were not supposed to cross string, as they just walked right over the string mashing it to the ground. After the string did not work your sister started to get on me to do something about those ducks as they cruise our yard from daylight to dusk looking for worms. Now I really don't think worms are on the endangered species list and at least when I walk in my yard a worm will zip down his hole before I step on one. However a duck dropping does not have the capability to do that as far as I know.

After much soul searching I came to the conclusion something had to be done about the duck situation because your sister and I like it here where we live and do not plan to move again. When I was farming I built a lot of fence over the years to keep our livestock confined, but I refuse to put up a fence here in town for someone else's pets. I would not think of alienating our neighbor's by complaining about their ducks, when I can handle the situation myself. As you know firing a gun in town is prohibited so shooting the ducks is out of the question. Trapping the ducks is next to impossible even though I did get get one accidentally in my squirrel trap a while back, I think I told you about that in my last letter.

Then I got to thinking those ducks like fish worms and I like to fish, so why not. I dug out my rod and reel and tackle box I had stored in garage the next day and tied a plastic worm on the end of my line, then I sat outside on my patio and waited for the ducks to come over in our yard. Finally they came over and I made a perfect cast right into the middle of the bunch. They started to fight over the plastic worm until one swallowed it, just like it was candy. I started to crank it in but was making no headway because I had forgotten to tighten up the "drag" on my reel. Before I could make the necessary adjustment on my reel, wouldn't you know my neighbor came out of his house with a bucket of shelled corn to feed his ducks. They knew he had food and started to take off on a dead run out of my yard and started swimming across his pond as fast as they could go. My fishing reel started to smoke the line was going out so fast, that is until it came to the end where it was tied to the spool on my reel. That caused the duck to do a back flip right in the middle of the lily pad patch in the pond. My neighbor's wife had planted the lilies in the pond and the neighbor says she thinks more of those lily pads than she does of him. Because she always shows them to everyone that visits and explains how hard they are to get started.

Now this duck with a plastic worm down its gullet is flopping and thrashing around in the lily pads and is getting the fish line all tangled up in the pads. My neighbor and I both get to the edge of the pond at the same time and I started to explain how I was practicing my casting in the yard when one of his ducks grabbed my line and took off with it. He started to take off his shoes and roll his pant legs up and said my duck will drown out there if we don't get it loose. So I reached in my pocket and took out my pocket knife and handed it to him and told him to cut the line when he got out there. He was wading out to about knee deep when his feet got tangled up in the lily pads and down he goes face first under water just about where the duck was. He comes back up spitting water and cussing like you never heard before, I was sure glad your sister was not out there to hear such words. He was still clutching my knife in his hand but he had lost the pipe he was smoking when he went out, that was probably the reason he was so mad. Then he stooped down to grab the duck and lost his balance again, however I give him credit he just went down on his knees this time. Since the water was only about three feet deep he still had his head above water, but the duck was flopping and splashing water in his face until he got hold of it. I could not see what he was doing under water, but I assume he was trying to get a good hold of the duck so he could cut the line. Then he started throwing lily pads right and left, he apparently was cutting them off with my knife in order to clear a space in the pads so he could find his pipe. I think he must love that pipe more than he does his wife, because I have never seen him without the pipe in his mouth.

About that time his wife came running out of the house yelling for him to get his rear end out of her lily pads. He said I lost my pipe in here and I am not coming out until I find it. Now I decided it was about time for me to get back in my own yard because I did not want to get mixed up in a family argument. I started to reel my fish line in and it felt like I had something on it, and I soon found out what it was. I was dragging about six inches of the ducks neck attached to the head across my yard. My good neighbor apparently made a huge error with my knife or else he became mad at the duck for making him lose his pipe. At any rate it appears that all three of us were losers, with my neighbor losing his pipe, I have not gotten my knife back yet and the duck lost its head.

Your sister said she had noticed the neighbor lady has not acted very friendly lately, so she did not want to ask her about the bare spot in her lily pads on the pond. Your sister also said she saw the neighbor digging a hole and it looked like he was burying a duck. I said maybe one got hit by a car when it was out in the street, you know they are running all over the neighborhood. Then I said to your sister, one down and three to go and your sister said shame on you.

Well I think I will close for now, sure wish you were here to go fishing with me tomorrow, especially now that I have all my fishing equipment out and working.

Till next time,   Your Sister's Husband

Dear Brother-in-law,

I think in one of my previous letters I had mentioned how many squirrels we have here in town. Your sister and I really like to see them occasionally and even feed them shelled corn but they are becoming somewhat of a pest burying things in our yard. The other day I counted twelve squirrels in our yard at one time, now I do believe we are being taken advantage of by the squirrels. We are running low on shelled corn but your niece came to our rescue by bringing about two bushels of acorns that she had picked up out of her yard from her big oak tree. I did not want to dump a big pile of acorns out so they could bury the excess for future use in our yard. So I decided to ration them out a few at a time so they would eat them instead of burying them.

I happened to remember an old sling shot down in the basement that the kids had years ago, so I dug it out and took a bucket of acorns along with the sling shot out on the deck in the back of our house. I saw this squirrel sitting in the yard about seventy five feet away, so I loaded up took aim and let it fly. To my amazement the acorn caught that squirrel square in the back of the head and he dropped like a rock, he was deader than a mackerel laying there in the grass. I kind of got a guilty feeling about that poor squirrel, but then it passed very quickly. After I carried the little fellow out of the yard and put it in the garbage can I decided to try a different tactic by lobbing the acorns up in the air. After a little practice I could drop one very close to a squirrel and they would look up in our sycamore tree waiting for more acorns to drop. I was having a lot of fun until I noticed; instead of eating them they were carrying them about fifteen feet away and burying them after digging a hole in our yard.

From then on I started dropping them closer to our neighbor's yard and the squirrel's followed right along, so I started lobbing the acorns over the shrubs into the neighbor's yard. I would estimate there were over a half dozen squirrels burying acorns like crazy before my bucket was empty. As near as I can tell he has about four hundred oak trees planted in his yard, I know my arm, thumb and forefinger got pretty darn sore. I guess I will have to wear gloves the next time I feed the squirrels. I read someplace that about half of the things that squirrels bury in the ground they never find to dig up again and that is how the forests get reseeded over the years.

One day while attending a garage sale a couple of blocks down from our house I saw a thing called a "Paint Ball Gun" that these crazy kids use to shoot each other, usually in the woods on weekends for recreation. The lady said her son had ordered it from a magazine several years ago and her husband refused to let him use it. They wanted to get the thing out of the house so I offered her five bucks and said I had a farmer friend that could use it to mark sheep with when he sorted them out for market. I really wanted to try it out to see if it would work for shooting acorns instead of using the sling shot that gave me a work out. I took the caps off a dozen acorns and loaded the gun and tried it out, however it did not work worth a darn. But I did get a box of paint balls that were red in color and I was curious how far the darn thing would shoot. I loaded up the gun with paint balls and was trying to decide where I could safely shoot it and finally I decided to just aim the thing up in the air and see what happened. The ball sailed up over a couple of trees and landed in the middle of the neighbor's pond scattering the three ducks that were on the pond, and the paint ball just sank to the bottom of the pond. Now I was in the Army Field Artillery in WWII and was on a gun crew where you used calculations to establish elevation and windage. I decided to use my knowledge to see if I could drop one in on a duck. I did get several hits and some near misses and it sure brought back some fond memories that I had while I was in the Army.

The next morning I looked out the window and then yelled for your sister to come and look at the neighbor's pond, it was red as a fire truck and the ducks were all red from the neck down. I quickly retrieved the box that the paint balls came in and I read on the box that they were "water soluble" and environmentally safe. Apparently over night they had evidently dissolved and mixed with the pond water making it look like a lake of blood. There was quite a lot of commotion going on at the neighbor's so I thought it best to stay away for the time being. That morning when the local paper came out, right on the front page it had a picture of my neighbor with his pipe between his teeth holding a Bible in his hands. The headline said, "City resident sees red" and the story goes on to say how a local man says the Lord has sent him a message and he proceeds to quote from the Bible, the book of Exodus, Chapter Six, Verse Fourteen how Moses said, "Let My People Go" before turning the waters of Pharaoh's Egypt red. My neighbor said in his case he will let his ducks go, and he hasn't missed a Sunday in going to church since that happened. It did cause problems for several weeks as people came from miles around to see the red pond. The city had to pay overtime for traffic control but the fast food establishments made a killing in town, so it all worked out O.K. Your sister found a red paint ball behind a chair out on the deck and wanted to know what it was and where it came from, so I had to confess up to what happened. Your sister is still giving me a hard time, but I pointed out to her that we do not have ducks in our back yard anymore. And with any luck we should have a woods full of oak trees close by in the future, if all goes well.

Well it is about time to wrap this up and by the way I just about forgot to tell you that our neighbor just called and invited us over tonight for a Bible Study Class that he is giving for the neighborhood.

Till next time' Your Sister's Husband.

Dear Brother-in-law,

I am sorry it took this long to answer your letter but we have been very busy keeping the lawn mowed with all the rain we have been having. Our neighbor that has the pond in his yard certainly has been having his troubles lately. I believe I have mentioned him in several of my letters to you and I think he is close to being eighty years old, but he moves around like a man in his nineties. The most strenuous thing he does every day is filling his pipe with tobacco and then striking a match to light it. Well several weeks ago he had a very close call with his lawn mower that ended up with him receiving a broken jaw. Now I know that sounds kind of hard to believe, so I will try to fill you in on the details.

As I understand it he pays his grandson that lives just next door to him to mow his yard; however he uses Grandpa's lawn mowers to do it. He cannot get too close to the pond with the riding mower, so he uses a hand push mower to cut the grass close to the pond. Well you know how the kids are these days when it comes to doing a little work. So Grandpa bought a new push mower equipped with a self propelled drive that can be engaged in or out with a lever on the handle. He though with a new mower his Grandson might be inclined to do a better job of trimming his yard with the new mower especially around the edge along the pond.

He was telling me this the other day when I went over to visit with him. I already knew pretty much what happened to him but I thought I would humor him by listening to his story anyway. He was very hard to understand; since he had his jaws wired shut until his broken jaw heals. He is on a liquid diet and has to use a straw that can be inserted into his mouth where a tooth used to be. He also has been able to smoke his pipe the same way, by unscrewing the end of his pipe and attaching a straw to it with scotch tape.

Apparently his Grandson was mowing the lawn that Saturday and was starting to use the new push mower when he became thirsty and went into the house to get a drink of water. The only trouble was he got to watching television and forgot he still had mowing to do. So my neighbor for some reason or other decided he would try out the new mower himself. Now your sister and I had just sat down in our patio for a few minutes to read the mail that had just been delivered. Our patio has a good view of the neighbor's yard and pond area and we saw him start the mower, which by the way started on the first pull. There was about a foot of grass along the water's edge of the pond that he was going to attempt to mow, he would push the mower toward the water and then pull the mower back. Your sister said that was very hard work for him at his age and suggested I go and finish the job for him. I was just putting my shoes on, when your sister hollered and I looked up in time to see my neighbor being dragged into the water by the mower.

He had evidently accidentally pulled the lever that put the mower in self drive as he was pushing the mower toward the water. When the blades of the mower hit the water they must have acted just like the propeller of a motor boat. The mower jerked him into the water before he could let go of the handle. His reflexes not being what they used to be at his age prevented him from letting go of the handle in time. He also may have panicked and froze, at any rate the mower was going across the pond cutting a path right through the lily pads. Old Gramps just kept hanging onto the mower handle, which in turn gave the mower the perfect pitch for a high speed run across the pond. I would estimate they were going ten to twelve miles per hour because my neighbor was making a pretty good wake. When the lawn mower hit the far pond bank and came to a sudden stop, my unfortunate neighbor proceeded to crash into the mower handle with his jaw. He just lay face down in the water until your sister and I rushed over and proceeded to pull him up on the bank. I shut the lawn mower off and then I heard my neighbor trying to say something, he was bleeding profusely from the mouth and the blood was running down his chin. He was saying something like, I aust mi pi uh autr, and he just kept repeating it over and over. Your sister ran back to the house to call 911 and I stayed at his side until the arrival of the ambulance. Then it dawned on me what he was trying to say, he had lost his pipe in the water, as I told you before he is never without his pipe.

Now as it turned out he not only lost his pipe but he also lost the upper plate of his false teeth. It seems when he went into the water along with the pipe in his mouth as usual, he came to the lily pads and his pipe caught on the lilies and proceeded to pry the upper plate of his false teeth loose, and they also were lost in the pond along with his beloved pipe. He was very lucky he was not wearing the upper plate when he hit the mower handle or he would have broken it as well. His Grandson, very eagerly I might add, waded around in the pond for two days before he found his Grandpa's false teeth and his pipe among the lily pads.

Well I had better close for now and go mow the lawn again; the squirrels have trouble finding what they buried in the yard if the grass gets too high.

Till next time,   Your Sister's Husband

Dear Brother-in-law,

You may have heard we had a very late spring up here this year, the weather has been cold and wet, now it has turned around and summer has finally arrived. I know I have written several times about our neighbor's that have the pond, but I don't believe I ever told you their names. They go by Clyde and Daisy and seem to be a very nice couple, but Clyde is about three quarters of the way over the hill. Now their pond is just loaded with bull frogs, almost every evening your sister and I sit out on the patio and listen to their croaking. I said to your sister one day that it has been a long time since we have had a mess of frog legs, do you think the neighbor's would care if I caught some to eat? Your sister said to me you will never know if you don't ask, so the next day I walked over and asked Clyde if I could catch some frogs out of his pond. He asked me how I was going to catch them and I told him I still had a frog gig that I had used years ago, and I would just walk along the edge of the pond with a flashlight at night. Clyde said he had a canoe in the shed and he suggested using that, because you can get closer to the frogs from the water. Old Clyde then volunteered to paddle the canoe and we could divide the frogs we caught fifty-fifty, that sure sounded fine to me but I did have the presence of mind to ask when he had last used the canoe. Clyde reckoned as how it would have been forty years ago when the kids were young, but said it was made of aluminum and should be as good as new. We decided to try our luck that night, so I went over to help Clyde get the canoe out of his shed. And that turned out to be not an easy matter because it had forty years of junk piled on top of it.

That night about nine o'clock we met at the canoe and rolled up our pant legs and took out shoes and socks off before sliding the canoe quietly into the water. I got in front with the frog gig and flashlight and Clyde got in the back with the paddle and a burlap bag to put the frogs in after I speared them. Old Clyde could handle the canoe fairly well considering his age, I would put the light on a frog and Clyde would maneuver the canoe in close so I could spear the frog. When I got one I would then swing the spear around to Clyde and he would pull the frog off and put it in the burlap bag. About half way around the pond I quietly asked him how many frogs we had by now and he said six or seven. I knew we had more than that and I figured he had just lost count during all the fun. Then I started to hear him giggle every so often like someone was tickling the bottom of his feet or something. Two frogs later I looked out of the corner of my eye and saw Clyde stuffing a frog in his shirt. After that I kept watching him on the sly and discovered he was stuffing about every third frog inside his shirt instead of putting it in the bag. It was very apparent he was giving me the short end of the stick, and then I remembered when we moved to town another neighbor had told me not to let anything lay around because old Clyde was known to have sticky fingers. I had let that go in one ear and out the other at the time, but now I realized we were actually living next door to a kleptomaniac. We were almost finished when a police cruiser pulled up in the yard and flashed his spotlight on us and demanded to know what we thought we were doing. I explained to the officer that we were frog hunting because the season had just come in, and besides we were on our own property, at least Clyde was. I also said that we did not need a license because we were both over sixty five. The officer informed us that hunting or fishing was illegal in town, and he proceeded to place us both under arrest, and started transporting us to the city jail in his cruiser.

Now can you imagine what it was like sitting in the back seat of a cruiser with someone that had live bull frogs stuffed inside his shirt? Clyde was giggling nonstop with those frogs squirming and crawling around his middle. I decided to confront him and I asked him why do you have frogs inside your shirt? He told me the bag got full and he didn't know where else to put them and then he started to giggle again. I started to laugh too and the more I started thinking about it the harder I got to laughing. The police officer turned around when he stopped for a red light and said I am going to give you both a breathalyzer test when we get to the station, the way you guys are acting.

At the police station they made us stand in front of a camera to take a mug shot, we still had our pant legs rolled up to our knees and we were still barefooted. The Sergeant at the police station said you guys look like you have been drinking to me and then he looked at old Clyde and said, you sure are acting like you are intoxicated to me. I could see Clyde's shirt moving with the frogs crawling around his waist, but with him being so skinny not one of the officers noticed anything unusual about him.

Then I heard a weird sound coming from Clyde's shirt, it sounded a little familiar but I just couldn't put my finger on it. There were three distinct sounds like, bud—wys—er, and then it hit me, the beer commercial on television. I got to laughing so hard I couldn't stop so they decided to test Clyde first, and he promptly blew a fuse or something on the machine. Clyde had been a chain pipe smoker for well over fifty years and evidently the machine blew out when it got a whiff of old Clyde's breath. I do know the next time we go frog hunting I'm going to set behind Clyde and I will do the paddling and sack the frogs.

Clyde just could not take it any longer, so he pulled his shirt out of his pants and eight frogs fell to the floor and started hopping around all over the police station. When everyone finally stopped laughing the Sergeant said call your wives to come and get you, and don't forget to take your frogs with you. Well Clyde's wife Daisy beat your sister to the police station and the first thing she said was, you sure smell fishy. I was surprised her nose was still that good since she has been married to Clyde for over fifty years.

We had frog legs for several meals and they were very good even with everything I went through to get them. Write when you can, also your sister says to tell you hello.

Your Sister's Husband

Dear Brother-in-law,

Well here it is another couple of months have gone by and I owe you a letter again. If I remember correctly in my last letter I told you about catching frogs with my neighbor. Since that time my neighbor Clyde and I have been fairly good friends, but I still would like to strangle his dog that barks all day long.

Clyde's Grandson that lives across the yard from his grandparents just turned sixteen years old several weeks ago. The boy wants to get his driver's license real bad, like all the kids do as soon as they reach sixteen. However both parents work and evidently are too busy to ride with him as he practices his driving with an adult, so Clyde told him he would help teach him how to drive. Now when Clyde told me this I said don't they have driver's education available for the kids, to teach them how to drive? He said yes but I think they need to know other things that are not taught, like defensive driving, and just using good old common sense. I knew he had his work cut out for him because I have watched this kid use the riding lawn mower for over a year now, a dozen sheep could do a better job on the lawn and in a lot less time. When I told your sister I thought Clyde was making a big mistake, she flat out told me it was none of my business.

Then this past week your sister and I were sitting out in the yard under a shade tree enjoying ourselves, listening to the birds sing. We saw Clyde and his grandson come out of the house and get in the car that was parked outside the garage. Now Clyde is about eighty years old and doesn't walk too well anymore, in fact he even shuffles his feet when he walks. Before he even reached the passenger side door of the car the kid had the car started and was revving the engine. When Clyde shut the door his grandson rammed the car in reverse before old Clyde got his seat belt fastened. I later learned that is how Clyde got his pipe broken again, when his head hit the dashboard. The kid then squealed the tires and burnt rubber as he took off down the street. I could clearly see old Clyde with his head pinned back against the head rest, with just a pipe stem sticking out of his mouth. The last I saw of them was when they went through the four-way stop intersection down the street without stopping.

About ten minutes later I heard tires squealing again and then saw Clyde and the kid sliding around the corner onto our street. They shot past our house and the gravel flew as they turned into their driveway. Luckily the kid at least did not try to put Clyde's car into the garage; instead he turned into the yard and slid on the grass to a stop under a tree. He jumped out and ran across the lawn to his own house and went inside. Apparently he was in a hurry to get to the bathroom or maybe his favorite television program was about to start.

Now Clyde was still in the passenger seat with his arms stretched out with his palms resting on the dashboard and I asked your sister if she thought Clyde was still conscious. Your sister said that he had probably passed out down by the four-way stop intersection a few minutes ago. It was about then I saw the car start to slowly roll down the sloping yard heading directly toward the pond.

Apparently the kid failed to put the car in park when he got out, and there was nothing we could do but to watch in dismay at the scene that was unfolding right before our eyes. Then I saw Clyde lurch for the steering wheel and desperately attempt to steer the car away from the pond. It was a matter of too little too late as the car settled down in the middle of the lily pad patch in about four feet of water. Clyde then opened the car door and stepped out into water up to his waist and threw away what was left of his pipe and then proceed to wade out of the pond. I quickly told you sister to cover her ears with her hands because I had heard Clyde cuss once before. However he must have picked up some new words since then because he was extremely upset and vocal as he fought his way through the lily pads and climbed up the pond bank.

But as I told your sister there is always a bright side to everything if you look hard enough, because when the tow truck pulled Clyde's car out of the pond. There were three large bass and seven blue gills flopped out on the grass when the doors were opened up. I tried to cheer Clyde up by offering to clean the fish for him but he says his mouth was too sore to be eating anything for a while; evidently he must have hit the dash pretty hard when he broke his pipe. He told me I could have the fish if I wanted them and I bet that nearly broke his heart when he had to give something away.

You know I am getting to like living in town more and more because it seems there is always something going on. As I look back now, living on the farm was rather dull most of the time. Well, your sister says dinner is ready, and you know it is best not to keep the cook waiting. So I will close for now and also the cook just said to tell you hello.

Your Sister's Husband

P.S. I almost forgot to tell you, we are having pan fried fish tonight, one man's misfortune is another man's gain they say.

Dear Brother-in-law,

Your sister and I were glad to get your letter last week; it's always good to hear your complaints about the hot weather down in Florida, Ha! Ha! However we are sorry to hear about your hemorrhoids flaring up again. I know how you enjoy eating out every evening down there, but maybe you should try eating someplace else besides "Taco Bell" every evening. I ate at one of those places one time and it really tore me up, if you know what I mean.

Remember in one of my previous letters I told you about our neighbor's and the various pets they own, well wouldn't you know Clyde and Daisy's daughter that lives next to them brought not one dog but two dogs home from the dog pound last summer. Unfortunately, and I say that with tongue in cheek, one of the dogs died soon after it arrived. However the other dog then became their house pet, which pleased us very much at the time because we could not hear his constant barking when he was outside. I think they named him spot; they probably came up with that name after looking at their carpet after several weeks with the dog in the house.

This past fall the neighbor's son-in-law got a new job that is quite a distance from town and it requires him to leave for work at the ungodly hour of four thirty in the morning. How do I know this, because when he leaves the house for work he lets their dog Spot out and then after the dog gets done doing what dogs do, he starts barking to be let back in the house. Now the dog continues to bark until around six o'clock when Clyde's daughter gets up and lets her precious darling back in the house. Now this does not affect me too much because I don't hear that well with my hearing aids laying on the dresser in the bedroom. However it is another story with your sister because she has excellent hearing and is a very light sleeper. The dog with his constant barking is causing your sister to lose about two and a half hours sleep every night. Therefore she needs to add that amount of time to the front end of her sleeping period.

This problem results in your sister falling asleep about eight thirty in the evening while I am still flipping through channels on the television trying to find something good to watch. Then if I want some popcorn, I have to go and pop it myself besides going again to get a diet Pepsi out of the fridge. She does wake up around eleven to watch the late news with me before we go to bed. I keep telling your sister to call up Clyde's daughter and tell her the dog barking is a neighborhood nuisance and if she does not do something about it you will call the police. But your sister wanted me to talk to the Mayor because on his weekly talk on the radio he says he will help anyone in the city with a problem. Besides your sister thinks I have some "pull" just because I went to city hall and complained about a "chuck hole" in the street in front of our house that was bothering your sister and they did fix it in a couple of days. So to keep your sister happy I talked to the Mayor about the barking dog problem and he assured me he would look into the situation because that was just one of the many facets of his duties as being Mayor of this fair city.

The very next morning about five o'clock in the morning your sister woke me up to tell me something was going on over at Clyde's daughter's house, because several police cars were parked in their driveway with their lights flashing. Just then it came over the police scanner that your sister likes to listen to, that an ambulance was needed at that address to transport the Mayor to the hospital. I then suggested to your sister that maybe she should go over and see what was happening, because the local newspaper never gets anything right anymore. She said she did not have high enough boots to wade through the snow in the yard. I was just about ready to suggest she could go around by way of the street, but thought better of it because your sister gets rather irritable when she don't get enough sleep.

The next morning I heard the story while drinking coffee up at the local coffee shop with a bunch of retired guys that call themselves the "Rusty Zippers". One of the guys there had talked to one of the police officers that had been on the scene. It seems the Mayor had been standing on the porch ringing their doorbell at five o'clock in the morning. Because he observed their dog barking to get back in the house, just like I had told him the day before. Spot however, had evidently refused to go off of the porch to empty his bladder because he apparently did not want go out in the deep snow. As near as we can ascertain the dog must have decided the Mayor's leg would be a good replacement for a tree and it was a lot handier so he started to relieve himself on the Mayor's leg. The Mayor at that point, and who could blame him, turned to kick the dog away and apparently slipped on the now wet porch floor landing on his back, injuring himself. I was told while the paramedic's was placing the Mayor in the ambulance he was overheard murmuring, be careful of my suit, be careful of my suit, the Mayor owns a clothing store and takes great pride to be a very neat and particular dresser, wearing a different suit every day.

Well I think I had better close for now, there is not really too much going on around here in the winter with all the snow and all. But I do think I will brave the weather and probably go up to the hospital later on today and visit the Mayor, I think I had told you before the Mayor and I are very good friends. Your sister just came by yawing and said to tell you hello, I think she just woke up from one of her naps again.

Till next time, Your Sister's Husband

Dear Brother-in-law,

I guess it's about time that I write you a letter again from up north. It sure is good to see grass starting to green up again, that means spring has finally arrived. Last week I was trimming a couple of limbs from the neighbor's tree that was hanging over our property line pretty low. Soon old Clyde our next door neighbor, who never misses a thing, came shuffling over to watch me work. During our conversation Clyde mentioned the tree in question was not good for anything and probably should be cut down. Thinking he was hinting for a free favor I suggested that I could cut the tree down and make firewood for their fireplace and haul the brush with my pickup truck out to the farm and dump it in the woods. And just as I figured old Clyde went for that, it would be worth the extra work just to get rid of that darn eyesore.

Two days later I brought the chainsaw in from the farm and started by sawing a couple of limbs that were in my way before starting down at the base of the tree. Out of the corner of my eye I saw Daisy running down the yard toward me in a gallop, yelling something but I could not hear her because of the noisy chain saw. I shut the chain saw down before she ran into it, then she proceeded to inform me that she did not want that tree cut down because it had white flowers on it, now most people would call them blossoms. By then Clyde came up all out of breath, so I pointed to him and said to Daisy that Clyde had wanted the tree cut down. She looked at Clyde and said did you tell him to cut the tree down? I was looking for him to shake his head up and down because he is hard to understand with his pipe in his mouth. Instead he shook his head back and forth so fast the ashes were flying out of his pipe, so much for who wears the pants in that family, no pun intended.

That brings me to tell you the story of the first time I met Daisy, over fifty years ago. A very good friend of mine, at the time, when I was a junior in high school asked me to go on a "blind date" with him. He would pick me up first then go pick up his girlfriend that went to the same high school his cousin went to, located about fifteen miles across the County from our school. I unfortunately agreed without first asking him if he had a picture of her or asking him if she was good looking.

On the evening of the date my so called friend, picked me up then picked up his girlfriend along the way to his cousin's house. When we got to his cousin's house I had to go up to the house alone because my friend was too busy necking with his girl friend in the front seat instead of introducing me to his cousin. When I knocked on the door I expected to see my date but instead her bald headed father came to the door and the first thing he said was, now I expect you to behave yourself with my little girl, you hear? Before I could answer this girl appears and her father said this is my little girl Daisy. Now I was about five feet eleven inches tall at the time and I found out later from my, so called friend, that Daisy was about six foot three and still growing. When she smiled her upper lip would slip up over her "buck" teeth, exposing her gum line above her teeth. She also giggled all the time, that is how she lost her chewing gum in the back seat of the car and then she lost it again later while trying to put it in her pocket before we ate popcorn in the movie.

While we were on our way to the picture show I tried to strike up a conversation with her since they were too busy up in the front seat to do any talking. I said to her I see your father raises hogs, and I knew that because I could smell hog manure when I was walking up to her house. Daisy just nodded her head, continuing on I said we raise hogs too, thinking that might loosen her up since we had something in common. That did get a smile out of her, exposing her perfectly spaced front teeth. After about another five minutes I asked her how many hogs her father had, and she just shrugged her rather broad shoulders. Five minutes later I decided to change the subject and asked her if she helped her dad do chores out in the barn. The reason I had asked her that was because she had on a pair of high-top work boots. The first word I heard her say that night was when she said ouch! when she hit her head as she was getting out of the back seat of the car.

During the movie she ate three bags of popcorn and drank two bottles of pop, I thought she might have trouble drinking from a bottle but she got along just fine. I would never complain about how anybody eats their food, but it was a little ironic how she ate popcorn out of the bag without using her hands. Everything was uneventful for the rest of the evening until we arrived at her house and I was walking her up to the door. Daisy accidentally stepped on my foot with one of her work boots and darn near broke my foot, I couldn't play basket ball for the next two weeks because of the severely bruised arch on my left foot.

I never saw Daisy again until we moved to town here some fifty years later and discovered we were neighbors. The years have not been kind to Daisy, she has filled out considerably, however she does not have those "buck" teeth anymore. There is just this empty space from one eye tooth to the other eye tooth; she must have collided with Clyde's pipe during a moment of passion. Getting back to the subject of cutting the tree that I was telling you about earlier. Clyde's pipe must have gone out during his head shaking and he went back to the house to refill it. Completely out of the blue Daisy asked me why I had never called her for another date, years ago. Now I have taken pride over the years to never tell a lie, but I didn't want to hurt her feelings so I decided this was the time for a little white lie. I told her I hit my head while playing basket ball a week after our date and had lost my memory for almost a year. I guess that done the trick because the subject never came up again. However she does wear shorts during the summer along with her high-top work boots when working out in her garden and I try my best not to look when she does that.

I really must close this letter as I am sitting out on the patio writing this and I just noticed my neighbor Daisy started to work in her garden again. You sister wants me to tell you she said hello and to be sure and write us when you can.

Till next time, Your Sister's Husband

Dear Brother-in-law,

Your sister and I received your welcome letter this past week and are so glad to hear the weather has been to your liking the past winter down in Florida. We have had very nice weather here the last several weeks and are able to set out on our patio and enjoy Mother Nature. Our neighbor had quite an experience the other day but I guess he has recovered because I saw him yesterday with a shovel and the wheelbarrow cleaning up dog piles in his yard. You may wonder why he would be doing that when he no longer has a dog of his own, so I had better back up and tell you what happened last week.

I think I told you before about his daughter that lives next door to him that has had a dog the last several years. They got him from the dog pound and this dog apparently was the result of a short love affair between some kind of a "bird dog" and probably a Mastiff, as near as I can tell because this dog is huge. Clyde's daughter and son-in-law both have jobs during the day and their kids are in school most of the day so Clyde offered to let the dog out of the house and walk him twice a day. Now I should say from my observations that the dog really walks Clyde because he could very easily be a member of a sled dog team up in Alaska the way he pulls old Clyde around the yard on his leash.

There also is no need for Clyde to hire a "lawn care" service to fertilize their yard anymore as Spot is taking good care of that job. Earlier this spring I thought the ground moles were working in their yard but later I discovered this was not the case ever since Clyde started walking the dog. My neighbor is no spring chicken anymore but I give him credit on his foot work while walking through his yard trying not to step on a dog pile. The lawn does look a little different with several shades of green mixed in with the bleached spots but that will probably even out once they start mowing their lawn. I shudder to even think about setting on a riding lawn mower trying to mow their lawn, I have spread my share of manure over the years on a dairy farm but I never used a lawn mower to spread it.

The other day I was out walking in the yard when I observed Clyde walking over to his daughter's house to take their dog out for his first of the day, bathroom call. Just as Clyde came out of the house with the dog a pair of wild geese landed on the pond, the dog seeing the geese immediately gave chase. Now Clyde apparently puts his hand through the loop of the leash to make it easier for him to hold on to it, but the dog apparently jerked so hard he could not let go of the leash quick enough when the dog lunged after the geese. Clyde was dragged clear across the yard face down but when the dog dived into the pond Clyde had other things to worry about, like holding his breath. Old spot kept going until he caught one of the geese by the neck right in the middle of the lily pads; I was about ready to holler for your sister to call the fire department because I did not see any signs of Clyde. Then I saw his head come up and he was spitting water or something out of his mouth, at least I thought it was water at the time. He was in a sitting position because the depth of the pond at that location was only four feet deep. The flopping goose still in the dogs mouth was splashing so much water it was hard to see what was going on but apparently the goose knocked Clyde down under water again because the next time I saw them, Clyde had the goose by the neck with his hand. Then the dog saw the other goose standing on the bank waiting for its mate, and took off again dragging old Clyde with the leash still wrapped around his wrist. When Clyde's head hit the bank of the pond he and the dog came to a sudden stop. Clyde just laid there part in the water and part out of the water, with his arm stretched out as the dog just kept pulling to get loose. I rushed over and pulled Clyde the rest of the way out of the water and took my pocket knife and cut the dogs leash from his wrist. In his other hand he was still clutching the goose by the neck which by now was a goner but old Clyde did not seem to notice that fact.

Now I can't tell you what Clyde's first words were because your sister always reads my letters before she mails them to you. I helped Clyde up to their house and rang the doorbell so Daisy could help him in the house. When she opened the door she just stared at him and said you look like something the dog just dragged in. That was when he swung the goose still in his hand hitting her across the side of the head telling her to shut up and stuff this damn bird for supper. At that point I made a hasty retreat back across their yard watching very carefully where I stepped. I went in the house and told your sister that she probably could get a good night's sleep tonight because there was no dog around to be barking any longer. Now I don't know what Clyde told his daughter about losing her house pet but I have noticed how he is smiling a lot more now. I can't help but wonder if he is happy because he has no dog to walk anymore or maybe in all the years of being married he has finally gotten the last word in for once.

Guess I had better close for now and go out and fill the bird feeder before supper. And by the way I almost forgot to tell your sister said to say hello and tell you to keep writing as she enjoys your letters.

As always,

Your Sister's Husband

Dear Brother-in-law,

It has been quite a spell since the last time I dropped you a line, but you know how it is during the summer months. We all are a lot busier during the summer months with the yard work and all. About two weeks ago we had a little commotion here in the neighborhood that could have turned out to be very serious.

As you know it has been very dry here this summer and our neighbor's pond has just about dried up. It has less than six inches of water in the deep end and where the lily pads are located it is only mud. I was reading the newspaper out on the patio when I observed our neighbor Clyde start out on his daily shuffle around his property. You can never predict what he might do on those journeys and I will proceed to tell you why I say that. He used to water his newly planted weeping willow trees almost daily, that his son had planted for him right on our property line in a twenty foot space between to big walnut trees. For some unknown reason both trees died over the winter, and wouldn't you know his son got him another pair and planted them at the same location. The next summer the trees were about three feet high and looked like they came from a river bank someplace. They were tied to a small stick that was driven into the ground to hold them upright and Clyde watered those suckers every other day all through summer just like clockwork. But for some reason or other they also died over the winter just like the ones the year before did. But Clyde continued to water them all through spring and summer even though they were dead. I could be mistaken but just last week I thought one of the stakes holding up one of the dead trees was starting to sprout from the top.

One evening this spring Clyde came down through the yard after the dandelions had gone to seed smoking his pipe as usual. He never picks up his feet but just shuffles when he walks and there was this big cloud of fluffy dandelion seed following him across the yard. Your sister said what is he going to do now? I told her I didn't have the foggiest idea. Then he stopped and took his "Zippo lighter" from his pocket even though his pipe was already lit. He bent over and proceeded to ignite a dandelion seed puff one at a time smiling all the while he was doing that. I told your sister if he intends to get rid of his dandelions that way he will need about a gallon of lighter fluid to finish the job. On the other hand he may have thought it was the forth of July and was just too darn tight to buy a few sparklers for the occasion, but then it was only the first week of June. You are the only one that we told this to because anyone else around here would think we were just making it all up.

Getting back to the little incident involving the pond I started to tell you about that took place a couple of weeks ago. One day I saw Clyde coming out of the house a little friskier than usual, he stopped at their almost dried up pond, sat down and started to take his shoes and socks off and rolled his pant legs up to his knees. He started walking through the mud out to the lily pad patch giggling as he watched the mud squish up between his toes. Then Clyde stooped over and started picking lily pad blossoms and then stuffing them in every one of his pockets. I figured it must have been Daisy's birthday and he was picking her a bouquet of lilies, as that would be her favorite flower. At any rate as he was stooping over picking blossoms, their old drake duck waddled over and nailed old Clyde right in the rear end. The duck must have been after a bug that was hanging on to Clyde's pants, anyway Clyde let out a yell and flopped over backwards as his feet were stuck in the mud. I ran over to the edge of the pond and asked him what he wanted me to do, and then I noticed his ears were full of mud and probably he could not hear me anyway. He kept yelling something and it sounded to me like, goin-kick-ducks-ass then he spit the pipe out of his mouth and then I understood what it was that he was trying to say. It was, get me out of this gooey stuff fast, so I went to the garage for my boots but Daisy must have heard all the commotion and she came out of the house to help Clyde. When I came back Daisy was in the mud trying to pull on one of Clyde's arms to get him up when she fell directly on top of poor old Clyde. At that point I understood something had to be done beyond what I could do, so I yelled for your sister to call 911 for the fire department for help. I couldn't help but think that this was probably the first time that Clyde and Daisy had been that close for years. When two members of our city fire department got there they waded out and rescued Daisy first, and she had a lily blossom sticking behind each ear and later when I told your sister about that she said you got to be kidding me. The firemen had a harder time with old Clyde as he was almost completely buried in the mud, and was pretty slippery for them to get a good grip on him.

After the fireman left and we went into the house it wasn't long before your sister hollered at me to come to the window and look. Clyde and Daisy were squirting each other with the garden hose and laughing and giggling around like crazy. The next day there was a big story in the local newspaper about how our two of our brave city fireman risked their lives rescuing a man that was lying on the bottom of his pond. Well, I had better close for now as it is about time for my neighbor's daily trip around his property and I don't want to miss anything. Your sister says to tell you hello and to write us when you can.

As always,

Your Sister's Husband

Dear Brother,

I usually let my husband write to you but he has been busy this spring working out on the farm and other things that I will detail later. I am sorry I missed your phone call the other day but I had gone away for the afternoon. I have to get away from the daily routine around here once in a while.

We went fishing this week out at our farm pond, the weather has been beautiful and we thought it would be nice to try our luck at fishing. You know me; I am used to fishing out of a boat where there are no trees or bushes. I spent more time untangling my line than fishing, and then I lost my bobber when I jerked too hard and it floated away. Your brother-in-law gave me his pole to use while he fixed mine back up by putting on all new equipment. We did catch a nice mess of large bluegills so we decided to bring them home to clean and eat.

You probably remember our neighbor's, Clyde and Daisy from all the stories my husband has told you about them. When we got home Clyde and Daisy were sitting out on their porch when we went to clean the fish out behind our large Sycamore tree. I knew they could not imagine what we were doing as we would stoop down each time we got a fish out of the bucket to scale and clean, each of us at different times. If you remember a few years ago when we were up at the camp ground at Lake Erie your brother-in-law was not too swift at cleaning fish. He said it was because he was left handed and he always had to use a right handed knife, at least that is the excuse he always used.

Your brother-in-law has been going turkey hunting the last several weeks because the season had just opened up in our County for the first time ever.

He has been getting up at five o'clock every morning in order to be out in the woods by sunrise, the hunting hours end every day at twelve noon. He always would have a big story about hearing a gobbler but could not call him in close enough to get a good shot. I finally asked him one day, what are you going to do with a turkey if by chance you do shoot one? He said we could dress it out just like we did the chickens, now can you guess how many chickens your brother-in-law has dressed out in his lifetime? None.

Would you believe on the last day of turkey season my husband shot his first gobbler, a nice beautiful twenty one pounder. He came in the house and got a butcher knife and his rubber gloves and a five gallon bucket and went out to the shed to gut it. I decided to take some water out because he did not think about that small item. We were doing this in the shed because our neighbor's were our in their yard watching on the sly what we were doing, just like they always do. When I got out to the shed with the water your brother-in-law had put the turkey in the five gallon bucket head first before gutting it. He was looking for the right place to make the incision and I informed him he could not gut it in the bucket, so we both worked to get the bird out of the bucket without damaging the feathers because your brother-in-law was going to get the turkey mounted. Did I forget to tell you we are not eating this bird because he has to take it to the taxidermist the way it is, except for the internal parts in order to have it mounted? I made the big mistake of telling him years ago after he shot his first deer that I would allow him to display on the wall only the first of any wild animals he shot. Since then it has been a pheasant, two large fish, a buffalo head and our pet Banty rooster he shot by mistake, (that is another story all by itself) and now he shot a turkey. Your brother-in-law put his rubber gloves on and proceeded to make the incision while I held the bird as instructed. He made a very small incision across the vent just like the taxidermist had told him to do, over the phone. If you don't know what the vent is, you should look it up in your dictionary. You guessed it your brother-in-law's hand was too big to reach in and pull the guts out, so you know who has the smallest hands in the family. I put the rubber gloves on and he held the legs apart and gave me encouragement from time to time, I sure am glad your brother-in-law decided to be a farmer instead of a surgeon. Can you imagine how you would feel getting your appendix removed by him, or worse yet, your hemorrhoids?

(Nine months later, because I miss-laid your letter)

I will just finish this letter before I send it to you, besides the story now has an ending. When the taxidermist called and said the stuffed turkey could be picked up my husband took one of his hunting buddies along to get the bird. His good friend suggested your brother-in-law should make a glass case to keep the turkey in so it would stay clean. He thought that would be a good idea as he had some wild cherry wood on hand, so it would not cost much except for buying the glass. After he got back from the glass shop he had a large mirror for the back side of the proposed case because they gave him a good price at $12.00. But the shatter proof glass amounted to $65.00 not counting all the fasteners that was needed to hold the glass to the frame. Your brother-in-law did a nice job making the glass show case, but then it ended up in our patio taking up a lot of room. It was there about a month and in that time several neighbors' came over to admire the beautiful turkey. One day I came home and it had been moved down to the family room in the basement. I have no idea how he got it down the basement stairs by himself. I asked him and he said it was worth the effort since he will not have to listen to my griping about it being out in the patio anymore.

Turkey season came in again a week ago just as it will every spring from now on, and you will not believe this but your brother-in-law was lucky enough to get his second turkey in as many years. And yes your brother-in-law tells me we are going to eat this one because he is sending for a "turkey cooker kit" he saw in a hunting catalog the other day. He went on to tell me they were on sale and cost only $97.00 including everything except the propane tank. We found a new propane tank at the "Lowe's Store" for $26.95 and he says he can fill the tank out at the farm from one of the propane grain drying tanks. He tells me there are a lot of ways to save money like that if you just use the old head that is on your shoulders. It looks like I had better mail this letter quick as you brother-in-law is heading out to the big Sycamore tree with a five gallon bucket, a butcher knife and his nineteen pound turkey. But it looks like he forgot to take water along with him again.

Love, Your Sister

P.S. Your brother-in-law had to re-order from the hunting catalog, as he forgot the "Uncle Bucks" peanut oil needed for the cooker. A four and a half gallon jug of peanut oil cost $29.95 also he ordered a screened funnel to re-jug the peanut oil for future use for only $4.95.

www.ingramcontent.com/pod-product-compliance
Lightning Source LLC
Chambersburg PA
CBHW061223280526
45784CB00006B/2613